# of the Deep

**IDF Andrew**

Cover painting: *'The Mirror'*, by Ingrid Andrew,
a self-portrait when a young woman.

Back cover art: *'Universe'*, by Ingrid Andrew,
an illustration for her verse drama,
*'When Woman created the World'*.

Published by William Cornelius Harris Publishing

In collaboration with London Poetry Books

*www.londonpoetrybooks.com*

Founded in collaboration with Second Chance

Supporting Mental Health in Performing Arts

ISBN  978-0-9932293-7-4

20 Spenlow Drive, Walderslade, Kent, ME5 9JT

W
C
H
P

# Contents

I am a Mermaid                                   Page   5

January's gift                                                   6

Every leaf is a green cup                             7

Through all the wild world's longing         8

Song of the Mountains                              10

The drowned world                                   12

The owl                                                      14

Nigella and her special guest!                     15

Macaron                                             16

How to write a poem                                 18

This Saxophone                                      20

Casper David Friedrich                         24

My daughter's first word was DARK        26

A FISHY ode                                    28

Afghanistan                                    31

The potato pickers                             32

The Loyal and Ever Lasting Umbrella            34

Ing's Ride                                     36

The Charcoal Woman                             38

Beast                                          40

The Surgeon                                    42

*The Author*
*Throughout her life, Ingrid Andrew created art and wrote poetry*
*prolifically. She later added music and song to celebrate her love*
*of the natural world and humanity, also her fears. Here you will*
*find quirky humour too and affectionate observation, but above all,*
*such tenderness. Ingrid died in 2015, but her creative website*
*www.ingridandrew.wordpress.com is still there to both stimulate*
*and soothe heart and soul.*

*Ingrid's first volume 'The Bird of Morning' is also available from*
*William Cornelius Harris Publishing.*

# I am a Mermaid

I am a mermaid *of the deep;*
I cannot walk, I may not sleep.

I'm a dark flicker in the blue,
to myself I'm always true,
I will not share my heart *with you.*

I am a mermaid of the deep;
I do not sleep, I cannot weep.
I'm swimming now in cloudy seas,
I like to sing, I like to tease.

You'll catch a glimpse of my womanly form
and then I'll leave you *quite forlorn.*

I am a mermaid of the deep,
my promises I always keep.
And ships may come, and ships may go,
and civilizations ebb and flow.

But I am promised to the deep,
that other company I keep;
when I catch a glimpse of *her* womanly form,
that's when I know … I'm truly home.

*I am a mermaid, of the deep.*

# January's gift

We are just at that moment when the evenings open up ~
when trees against pale turquoise and orange skies are like
inky paper cuts; when along the old avenue the street lights
come on one by one, like bright snow drops.

And shadows grow longer and richer, and hold the promise
of days to come.

When January, harsh and unforgiving after the tinsel and
comfort of December, is opening up a sky that every day
lessens a little the iron grip of night; a sky that in its
immensity can hold all our sufferings and anguish, and
all our sorrows.

Now January is the surprising gift, if in austerity embraced,
returns us to the growing of the light!

January shows us what must come ~
always transience, inevitable sorrows.

But when resistance softens and lets go,
here you are carried into the new year, through January,
until one lightening winter afternoon
in the top-most branches of still dormant trees,
you'll hear the small birds sing;
you'll sense the excitement of rebirth,
and the first, faint glimmerings of Spring!

# Every leaf is a green cup

Every leaf today is a green cup,
raised in thank fullness to the rain.

Every branch, every twig is lined with rain drops,
glinting silvery on the pale sky.

Every leaf is a green cup.

As I rest on the solace of my bed
with the blue grey curtains pulled aside,
and I let my self *dissolve.*

As rain keeps falling from the blank, white sky.

I could live here forever
with the murmuring of the radio,
the butterfly I drew in stained glass inks
upon the window.


*Every leaf is a green cup.*

# Through all the wild world's longing

I walked into my sorrow,
I walked into my longing,
I walked where the wind caressed the grass
in search of a belonging.

I walked beneath September skies
and through the rustling trees,
to see if I could rise again from where I'd fallen
on my knees.

I felt my heart's confusion; I felt my poor hearts pain.
I made a promise to myself, I shall love you, again.

Through all the great world's yearning,
the yearning and the longing, I shall fold you softly in.
I shall bring you to belonging.

And as I walked through this falls blond field
I was asked to bend and yield.
I broke the brittle mask I wear,
and stamped it on the earth to expose the tenderness within.
I was broken ~ for rebirth.

*I was broken for rebirth.*

And I asked that my heart be opened,
I asked that my heart could sing;
and I asked the gods of earth and sky
to mend my broken wings.

And I made a promise to myself,
to the frightened child inside~

I shall not abandon you. I shall with you abide.

*I shall not abandon you. I shall with you abide.*

I shall with you at last, abide,
through all the wild world's longing, child.

*Through all the wild world's longing.*

# Song of the Mountains

They are tearing down the mountains where the wild birds sang,
they are burning down the forests where the huckleberries grew,
they are pushing out the old souls who lived on and loved the land,
they are mining for the coal seams because we think
we need the fuel.

And the mountains and the trees that grew over centuries
are levelled and burnt down, and the little country towns
are filled with ash and dust, and the rivers and the streams
where fishermen once dreamed are poisoned and laid waste.
*What's to become of us?*

And where once the eagles flew, and gazed down on green and blue,
and the early morning mists curled round, caressed and
kissed the mountains, trees and streams;
there is nothing left to see, not a river, not a tree,
where they are levelling the mountain tops,
and burning down the forests
*to mine coal for you and me.*

We thought that mountains would endure,
and the air stay fresh and pure,
where illuminated trees stir within the gentle, evening breeze.
But now from sky to sky, just nothing meets the eye
except the wastes of ash and dust
where they are levelling the mountain tops,
and burning down the forests
*to mine coal for all of us.*

And just as all the small birds choked,
shrivelled up in flame and smoke, and their songs are silenced now,
so may we all one day perish
because we do not cherish
*this extraordinary world.*

Mountains of a million years, with all their diverse life and trees,
have fires set amongst their leaves, then the top soil is removed,
and explosives laid in grooves and the mountains blown away,
and nothing's left except thin stubble,
and the valleys fill with rubble,
and the rivers toxic waters poison
mothers, fathers, sons and daughters.

We do not know what life is worth.
What are we doing to
the good earth?

*What on earth?*

They are tearing down the mountains where the wild birds sang,
they are burning down the forests where the huckleberries grew,
they are pushing out the old souls who lived on
and loved the land,
they are mining for the coal seams
*because we think we need the fuel.*

# The drowned world
## (a song)

I'm sitting on the edge of the drowned world,
combing my seaweed locks,
perched on these slippery rocks,
slapping my fine, scaly tail at the odd, passing whale.


While the human detritus floats by
under these clear blue skies,
so many drowned souls,
and I think I just heard the last child's cry.......


Way down below me I see mountains, cities, tiny spires.
And now I hear the voices of the last drowned choirs.......


while
I'm sitting on the edge of the drowned world,
combing my seaweed locks,
perched on these slippery rocks,
slapping my fine, scaly tail at the odd, passing whale...

When the first icebergs began to melt,
I was very clear about what I really felt,
so just for a start...
I bought myself a brand new titanium heart...


Can you hear it ticking? It never loses time,
and the best thing about it is I feel just fine.


Sitting on the edge of the drowned world.

I while away the time here, I hum away the hours;
I can't even say I miss the grass and trees and flowers,
while I'm sitting on the edge of the drowned world,
all day long, and all night long,
singing my heartless, heart less, song,
now that everybody's gone,

*on the edge of the drowned world ......*

# The owl

The boy has caught an owl from deep within the forest.

He's tethered its large, pale yellow claws,
and holds it out, for fifty thousand,
as pet or meat.

Its large and heavy intricately feathered head
hangs down,
its body punctured and slack.

'Let it go.' the kind man said,
'Give it back to the wild where it belongs.'

The young boy smiles in innocent ignorance.

There
is no empathy

*in his distended belly.*

# Nigella and her special guest!

No apron she, this kitchen queen;
this goddess of the hearth.
This woman with her shapely arms,
and marvellous captivating bust!

This woman who flicks her insect eyes,
her head, to glance at the camera she lives inside,
to flirt with all of us!

Who never loses self-consciousness.
Even when she throws her head right back,
and laughs, laughs, laughs!

Who makes wealth seem like the natural order of things,
who never seems to question how luxury arrives...
or at whose expense.

I love her generous curves, the sensuous way she moves,
the way she likes to emphasise some words like *baste*
and *whip* with her full lips' caress.

I like her own self tenderness.
I hate her deep complacency...

But maybe she's an all-round winner!

Perhaps she invites John Pilger round for dinner!

# Macaron

I am in paradise; I am in heaven,
in a little patisserie called 'Macaron'
near Clapham Common.

The floor is parquet wooden,
the high blue ceiling is afloat with clouds,
two fat cherubs and
a cluster of lamps made from frosted ice;
and Bing is singing...

*'When you're young at heart,'*

And suddenly I am transported,
after all the petty disappointments and grievances of work;
I feel young at heart.

One waitress is as pretty as you'd expect,
she wears a girlish blue and white gingham dress,
so is the other, from Laos.

*(When the rhythm starts to play;*
*hold me close ...)*

I'm sitting at a broad wooden veined table,
a huge glass oval bowl of white, scarlet and
pink veined orchids just near me.

Come in, come into heaven.

Taste one of these little mango and orange cakes
as sweet as they need to be,
like a jewelled eatable
that Monet might have munched
before he went out to paint the trees,
heavy with their summer leaves.

Outside there are people sitting on the grass,
they could be made from Seurat's painted dots.
This could be Paris before the wars,
before the weather became permanently unstable,
before we knew the history of sugar.

Go on, come in, pretend with me,
that this is a sweet eternity, without cholesterol
or stiffening limbs, or loss or sorrow;
where it's always
mid-afternoon
and time for tea, and no tomorrow.

Just sweet sensuousness and innocence and peace,
in paradise,
in Macaron,
in heaven, where…

*'everybody loves somebody sometime.'*

17

# How to write a poem

*Firstly* let it all go,
your observations, thoughts and feelings and insights
just let 'em *flow*
and write and write and write and write!
If necessary far into the night.

And *then* pretend
that you are someone quite uptight!

Revise, revise, revise, *pare down,*
consider if every word is good enough
for your exalted piece;
get rid of all unnecessary *adjectives*
and then pare down some more!
Until your fingers on the scissors feel quite sore!
*Throw down the adverbs, clichés and worn out words
onto the kitchen floor!*

Until there's just the essential left
and even if you feel *bereft,* cut out the *rest!*

At last you're left with nothing
but a *simple empty page* that's full of space.
*Just like the one you started with,*
but more *erased!*

Don't be disheartened or depressed!

You've made a hymn of praise to the universe
*which now we learn* is

full of pulsing

emptiness!

# This Saxophone

While I was still unknown to myself,
this instrument *found* me.

In Berne I learned to play the *saxophone,*
before I even knew its sound...
Listened to Manu Dibango; still adored ~

Now here I am.
Wandering down cobbled streets, it's *night*
and I can hear a *lone* saxophone playing,
(deeeeep breath)

(knock, knock)

'I muss lehre saxophone spiele,
Chasch du mir zeige?'

(Listener, I learnt.....)

Next thing, I'm travelling all over Germany and Switzerland,
anywhere where *'Ich liebe dich, liebe mir'* is playing...

And the company's parting gift is the saxophone itself.
*(They recognize a love affair, when they see one.)*

I treasure it still,
though this one here is a Yamaha 62 Tenor Horn.
Now back in England, can't find acting work;
*disheartened* I head for home for the Welsh hills,
and on Shaky Bridge near Cefnllys Church
where troubled youth found *solace,*
I attract an audience of cows with my *looooong mournful notes.*

Solitude's gift.

I return to the city with what is described as this
'hauntingly high, marvellously mellow tone'
I'm booked straight away,
*Elation!!!!*
until thrown pages of complicated tadpole script:
'Go away and have some babies.'

So I did.

Ahhh, the *juggling* of all my loves;
my girls and my saxes, and here I am again, *rushing* for a train,
two children in tow, two saxophones shouldered, one daughter's
*crying,*
bend down to comfort her, and WHACK ~ bloody sax case!!!
but no damage done and at least she's just gone quiet...
(funny thing that, how my girls have never been that fond
of my music!)

Most temperate friend!
Respecter of all the heart's secrets,
revealer of truths,
surprise me again and again,
my confidante that moves with me,
and moves me, bends notes
and shakes the trees ....

To hell, with comparisons, my sax says,
with competition, exams, influences,
you ought to be listening to this....
have you heard of ?? ....

21

Saxophone says: I'll have none of that.
I'll show you this womanly path that unfolds as you're playing.
In me, you'll find true self, authentic voice.

Now here I am in the shed, my husband's *true love gift*,
a little soundproofed, away from neighbours,
here I can *meander,* bellow, blow quiet or sharp
explore the endless tributaries of *mellow...*

how easily my fingers *slip* into place,
my body adjusts to this weight,
cool metal caress, that warms to my touch...

Here I can play, and while marigolds take over the flower beds,
I learn the diminished chord and to an unfolding hyacinth's
heady scent.
I master the chromatic scale...

While in this trance, the season's everlasting dance goes on.

Stay down, stay down,
close to the mother pearl buttons for speed; where
Egyptian, golden Adonis figures clamber up the mechanism,
lending their strength to open and close the portals of pitch...
What I love best...

*(deep pause)* is

here and now
in a street or room to *respond;*
and as my breath expands,
to pick up a feeling from the air,

to catch a yearning, melancholy, a sweet telepathy
that liberates us all from *daily* cares;

sadness as deep
as deep
as deep
as *grief*

or joy that bubbles and *ascends* to the bluest sky
with marvellous clouds, like a *new morning* in the mountains

a rising *ecstasy* of *feeling*

then lets us
fall ....

fall ....

fall ......

beyond *seeing, hearing* and even... feeling,

to the pure essence

of what we share with all life

and that is simply the ground of

BEING ...

Written with saxophonist Vivienne Soan

# Caspar David Friedrich

There is a monumental stillness to his work;
a distilled ecstasy of being.
He shows us how the heart within the mind
has its own clarity of seeing.

Here, where the light defines
the great bell of the sky,
this painter,  from another age,
sees with a seer's, a poet's,
a lover's eye.

With his fine brush
he recreates each branch,
lovingly imitates
the particular bole of every tree,
the plains, the waves, the lush of grass,
the eternal, high and endless vista
of a midnight sky.

A solitary bird that's lost in flight.

And often, arm in arm some friends,
or a lone figure,
stands in reverie;
looks on, and is a part of everything.
Out to the mountain's brimming majesty,
across a broad and wrinkled, becalmed sea,
exalted by the rising moon,
the huge encroach of night.

And oh! the light, the light,

the light,

the light,

the Light!

# My daughter's first word was DARK

My daughter's first word was DARK, then MOON.
at three years old she said, *you cannot see your eyes.*

Now she is beautiful as Nefertiti was;
her laughter could reach the zenith of all the skies.
*She wants to be an astrophysicist.*
My God, she understands *physics!*

Will she be as unvain as the cosmologists who care not
for their own appearances *for their eyes are on the stars of time?*
In a dream I named her Rosa. I see her gazing from the
bejeweled earth out into *universe after universe.*

Will she study the novas, supernovas, galaxies,
the horsehead nebula and the 'question mark',
the yellow and blue and red and pale white stars?

She will understand dark matter, dark flow,
how there is an unseen energy in the spaces
*of what appears to be empty.*

She tells me about space: how we are mostly *emptiness*,
how huge our cells are,
*like football fields with a flea at the centre;*
she will learn about the dark energy *that flows through
being and nothingness.*

St John of the Cross talks of the *dark ray of light,*
and will my lovely beloved bright funny beautiful
sceptical daughter maybe see this colossal ever expanding
invisible energy, maybe one day, as God?

My daughter's first word was DARK,

her second word was MOON.

# A FISHY ode

Oh,
Did you know that when fish die,
they turn their faces to the skies?
they exude long, pain-filled sighs,
and sometimes have a little cry?

It may not seem quite right to you,
but fish have feelings, fish feel blue;
I can assure you *this is true!*

Sardine, pilchard, haddock, bream,
they are not cold fish, as they seem.
Just before they're going to die,
they turn their faces to the skies,
and emit soft little cries!

You wouldn't know it but they weep
to leave their home in the deepest Deep.

They cry a little before they die, because they love their
fishy lives, *like we love our lives, you and I.*

O o o o    ooooo o o why were we fish born at all,
except to feed our fellow fish or to end up on a dish?

And if you think this can't be right,
and it keeps you up at night,
worrying about fishy pain; *let me tell you once again ~*

fish have feelings, fish can cry,
and none of them feel glad to die.
My best friend told me, so it's true,
and I love her through and through.
If you knew her, so would you!
She just told me, *so it's true!*

It's something she has known for years,
the seas are full of fishy tears,
and fishy sighs and fishy cries,
and fish that wonder why oh why are our lives
so brief and small?
and why are some fish long and tall?
and some so gorgeous, some so plain?

Oh why oh why?! they cry again,
are some fish fat and some fish fin?
and some fish uglier than sin?
and some shaped like hot water bottles?
or covered in weird warts and wobbles?
And some have great extended eyes,
and some are modest and so shy,
while others roam the seven seas,
in search of fellow fish for tea.

And some hide on the ocean bed,
pretending they're asleep or dead,
while others hide in great sea weeds,
extend proboscii for a feed;
and some turn suddenly from blue
to a colour of a different hue
that you have never ever seen
even in your weirdest dreams.

Oh fish have feelings, fish can cry,
they turn their faces to the skies,
and often wonder, why oh why?

And some of them may live for years
and even smile through fishy tears.
And indulge themselves in fish ballet,
of jellyfish and huge stingrays,
and by midnight they're all asleep,
with eyes wide open, in the deep.


My dear friend is no scientist
and has been by fortune kissed.
For after all she's not a fish!
And lots of people love her dearly
and want to see her monthly, yearly.
She loves her children, husband, a dog called Ronnie,
and her outlook is mostly sunny.

*And do you know, her favourite dish,
is lightly sautéed flying fish?*

# Afghanistan

In his own language, and then, next to it in English:
*'heart grief'* then *'swelling'* *'abdomen'* and
*'it is sunny today'*, curling across the page, beautiful,
meandering, mysterious to me.

And he, so dignified, sitting quietly,
ponderous, handsome lined face,
black suit, tie-less white shirt.
He tells me his five children are all here;
his wife is ill. *'Depression'*

*'Afghanistan, great country, trouble country'*

He ran the Education Department, with 200 offices,

*'or the womans education. And the womans teachers.'*

*'Womans is very important. Womans is very important.'*

he says to me urgently.

*'This is first home for all of us, in woman's womb.'*

Now, he sits here quietly observing
in this simple church's living room.
*'heart grief'*

# The potato pickers

The potato pickers in dreary clothes
still smile at us, from the old photographs.
Beautiful, in their greys and whites and blacks;
one woman grins as she bends over heavily.

In their old clothes they line the furrows,
or throw the potato harvest onto trucks,
potatoes still stuck together by fibrous roots and dirt,
the pickers work, and laugh.

The photographs are old; and next to them
are water colours of different potato sorts,
and showing the bulbous roots,
growing from the clear cut watery half,
stuck in the ground by grimy hands that reek of earth.

And then the delicate, pale-white flowering plant.

My friend and I look up at the photographs, eat ice cream;
we're not hungry enough for the baked potatoes
in their little polystyrene bowls,
to pierce the papery skin
and fork the hot, floury tuber into our mouths.

In the small, dazzlingly bright kitchen,
two young women are almost too tired to speak;
and we know that the potato pickers are long gone,
laughing together in their grimy clothes,
their red hands caked with dirt.

We think of the huge and empty fields that yield their crops
to huge machines.

Out we go into the night,
still dazed from the day's long heat;
a strange disfigured moon, peeps from the ragged clouds,
the city trees are very full,
and still.

# The Loyal and Ever Lasting Umbrella

I'm making an umbrella that will last; that will faithfully
follow you home when it's mislaid or lost.

That has a real curving, comfortable handle made from
sustainable wood. And a design and colour that changes
with the weather *and your mood.*

On a summer's day it will be like a little piece of a heavenly sky,
that shelters you from a sudden downpour,
when the odd rain cloud *comes floating by.*

And in the fall it will be there to protect you,
*from a sudden squall.*

In winter when you're shivering while waiting
for a bus or train, it will surround you with a radiant heat
from the top of your head to your poor, cold feet.

And in the Spring it will light you up, as bright and sunny
*as a buttercup.*

And should you be bored and disconsolate and
longing for a ride,
this little umbrella at your side,
will take you up and very high,
into a lucent, *blue, blue sky.*

Like a magic carpet, or the red balloon, over the earth,
so *wunderschön.*
Will release you from all your worries and cares,
while you're free as a cloud in the bracing air.

*And spread out before you far below,*
*you'll see the Earth and see it rise,*
*majestic and marbled blue and white*
*and radiant in the Sun's great light.*

# Ing's Ride

I am Ingrid.  I am *Ing's ride.*  I *ride* the chariots of Spring.

I scatter petals in my wake,
and gather birds
and throw them on the wing.

I am the herald of the growing light.
I am the waker of the seeds.

I am the heart of life on earth.
I ride the fields and surf the wild and gentle winds.

I blow the beauty of the earth into your eyes.
I plant the seeds of beauty in your heart.

I give these seeds a name, I call them yearning,
I am here at the world's turning, turning.

Longing is what I call these seeds,
I love the wild flowers and the weeds.

I am the fierce and fertile mother,
of all the universe I am one lover.

I am Ing's ride,  I am the harbinger of Spring,
I ride the chariots of Spring.


And when man's reign is over with and done
in some far future millennium,
I will arise again in a sweet breeze
*and scatter petals through the trees,*
*and gently wake the sleeping seeds,*

for I am Ing's ride,  I am Ingrid.

I ride the chariots of *Spring.*

# The Charcoal Woman

The charcoal woman *rises* from the land.

Here, in the burning bush is where she stands.

Her smouldering head is turned toward the hills;
her body is rooted in the ashen soil.

Her torso is ebony and deep deep blue;
her broken and splintered back
is where the light comes through.

*Her breast is cobweb thin.*

She can no longer hear the magpie's lyrical morning song...
or ever again, the anguished cries of women and children.

Yet

here she stands, risen again from the land
in the country of cars and chainsaws.

In her womb is a brown seed.

In her womb is a brown seed that will *flame* into a green leaf.

*The charcoal woman rises from the land*

Ingrid was profoundly affected by the devastation
and desolation following wild fire in the Australian bush,
but inspired by the knowledge of renewal and new life.

# Beast

I shall *ride* you
BEAST!

Although you plunge me into abysses,
across the terrifying crevasses, towards
*sheer precipices*

I shall ride you
BEAST!

And when you try to throw me off,
to trample me, and eat me,
I shall show you that you cannot beat me.

**BEAST.**
Wherever it is you take me,
though your fierce heart
wants to consume me,
rake me into the ashes,
you shall *not* undo me.
You shall *not* unmake me.


**BEAST.**
On your broad back
I'll course the shadowed lands,
on your broad back one day I'll stand
and feel the wind run through me.

In quiet, sunlit pastures one fine day,

*you'll be eating gently*

*from my hands.*

# The Surgeon

The goodness of the man shines in his eyes.
Lathering his strong hands with yellow soap, he says,
'I feel I could do, I should do more.'

Speaks gently to a girl with a shattered arm,
to a bus driver he's helping to fit with a prosthetic leg,
(caught in an explosion, helping protesters to safety)
to a young boy whose face is covered in papery scars.

The young boy tells him that the scars hurt,
'but only at night.'

Bone from a young man's arm is transplanted to his leg
although he's tried to kill himself three times
(his wife and young daughter were killed in front of him)
'I am in constant pain' he says, and smiles.

'I worry more about their psychological injuries,'
the surgeon says,

'…. without this hospital there would be no sanctuary
for these wounded souls.'

While here, we augment or reduce our breasts,
have fat sucked out of our bellies, fret about lines...
and forget that our second biggest export is *armaments.*

www.ingramcontent.com/pod-product-compliance
Lightning Source LLC
Chambersburg PA
CBHW060526110426
42741CB00042B/2784